Big Cats

Cougar

Written by
Tatiana Tomljanovic
and Megan Cuthbert

MEDIA ENHANCED BOOKS

AV2 BY WEIGL™

ADDED VALUE • AUDIO VISUAL

www.av2books.com

AV² provides enriched content that supplements and complements this book. Weigl's AV² books strive to create inspired learning and engage young minds in a total learning experience.

Your AV² Media Enhanced books come alive with...

Audio
Listen to sections of the book read aloud.

Key Words
Study vocabulary, and complete a matching word activity.

Video
Watch informative video clips.

Quizzes
Test your knowledge.

Embedded Weblinks
Gain additional information for research.

Slide Show
View images and captions, and prepare a presentation.

Try This!
Complete activities and hands-on experiments.

... and much, much more!

Go to **www.av2books.com**, and enter this book's unique code.

BOOK CODE

X608762

AV² by Weigl brings you media enhanced books that support active learning.

Published by AV² by Weigl
350 5th Avenue, 59th Floor
New York, NY 10118
Websites: www.av2books.com   www.weigl.com

Library of Congress Cataloging-in-Publication Data
Tomljanovic, Tatiana.
 Cougar / Tatiana Tomljanovic.
   pages cm. -- (Big cats)
 Includes index.
 ISBN 978-1-4896-0914-4 (hardcover : alk. paper) -- ISBN 978-1-4896-0915-1 (softcover : alk. paper) --
ISBN 978-1-4896-0916-8 (single user ebk.) -- ISBN 978-1-4896-0917-5 (multi user ebk.)
 1. Cougar--Juvenile literature. I. Title.
 QL737.C23T633 2014
 599.75'24--dc23
                          2014004618

Printed in the United States of America in North Mankato, Minnesota
1 2 3 4 5 6 7 8 9 0   19 18 17 16 15 14

032014
WEP150314

Editor Heather Kissock   Design Terry Paulhus

Contents

Meet the Cougar

Cougars are **mammals** that belong to the cat family. In fact, the cougar is the second-largest cat in North America. Only the jaguar is larger. Cougars are predators. This means they hunt other animals for food. Cougars watch their **prey** from a hiding spot. Then, they follow the animal. This is called stalking. When the cougar is ready to attack, it will pounce on its prey.

Unlike some animals that eat both meat and plants, cougars eat only meat. They will eat any animal they can catch, from mice to deer or elk. Cougars live all over North America and South America. They prefer to live alone and are rarely seen by people in their natural **habitat**.

Cougars are shy and solitary animals. They are rarely seen by humans.

All About
Cougars

Cougars belong to a group of animals called *felidae*. There are 41 **species** of *felidae* in the world today. This group includes all cats, from lions to house cats.

Cougars are found in South America, western North America, and a small part of Florida. They live as far north as the Yukon, in Canada, and as far south as the Andes Mountains, in South America.

Cougars are known by many names. In fact, the cougar holds the **Guinness World Record** for the animal with the most names. Cougars have more than 40 names in English alone. Some of these names include mountain lions, pumas, panthers, and mountain screamers.

Cougars are sometimes called painters because the tip of their tails looks like it has been dipped in paint.

Comparing Big Cats

The cougar is the fourth largest cat species in the world. The tiger, lion, and jaguar are all larger than the cougar. Each of the cat species varies in size and speed. Some big cats rely on the power of their large bodies to help them hunt and catch their prey, while others rely more on their speed.

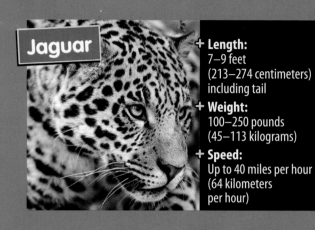

Jaguar
+ **Length:**
7–9 feet
(213–274 centimeters)
including tail
+ **Weight:**
100–250 pounds
(45–113 kilograms)
+ **Speed:**
Up to 40 miles per hour
(64 kilometers
per hour)

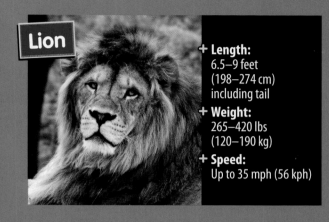

Lion
+ **Length:**
6.5–9 feet
(198–274 cm)
including tail
+ **Weight:**
265–420 lbs
(120–190 kg)
+ **Speed:**
Up to 35 mph (56 kph)

Tiger
+ **Length:**
7.5– 10.8 feet
(260–330 cm)
including tail
+ **Weight:**
220–675 pounds
(100–306 kg)
+ **Speed:**
Up to 40 mph (64 kph)

Leopard
+ **Length:**
6.5–9 feet
(198–274 cm)
including tail
+ **Weight:**
66–176 lbs (30–80 kg)
+ **Speed:**
Up to 57 mph (92 kph)

Cheetah
+ **Length:**
6–7 feet
(183– 213 cm)
including tail
+ **Weight:**
77–143 lbs (35– 65 kg)
+ **Speed:**
Up to 70 mph
(112 kph)

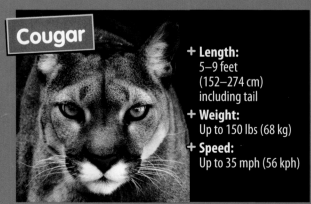

Cougar
+ **Length:**
5–9 feet
(152–274 cm)
including tail
+ **Weight:**
Up to 150 lbs (68 kg)
+ **Speed:**
Up to 35 mph (56 kph)

Cougar History

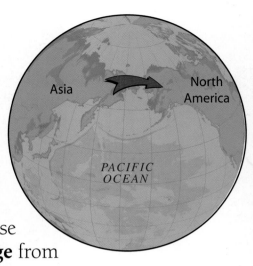

An **ancestor** of the cougar first came to North America about 8.5 million years ago. Some scientists believe these animals came across the **Bering Land Bridge** from Asia. They thrived in their new North American home. Over time, these cats spread farther across the continent and into South America.

Cougars had plenty to eat in the Americas, and their only **predator** was the wolf. However, Europeans posed a threat when they began settling the land. Cities and farms left less land for cougars to roam. Europeans also hunted cougars for their coats.

Cougars were hunted nearly to **extinction** in eastern North America. Only a small group remained in Florida. In recent years, the cougar population has begun to increase eastern North America.

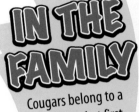

IN THE FAMILY

Cougars belong to a cat family that first lived in Asia about 11 million years ago.

There are about 16,000 cougars living in nature in North America.

Where Cougars Live

Cougars live in all major types of habitat in the United States. They can be found in river valleys, deserts, swamps, forests, prairies, and mountains. Sometimes, cougars take shelter in caves and thick bushy, grassy areas. They are often found in areas with plenty of rocky ledges or small hills. This is so they can pounce on top of their prey from high above.

The place where cougars roam and hunt is called a territory. Male cougars have territories that cover between 30 and 386 square miles (78 and 1,000 square kilometers). The territory of a female cougar is only about half this size.

Cougars have the largest range of any land mammal in North America.

HIDING OUT

Cougars are skilled at hiding among rocks, trees, or tall grasses. They do this so that they can surprise their prey.

Cougar Features

Cougars are very good hunters. They have special **adaptations** to help them stalk their prey. Cougars have powerful bodies, and the color of their fur helps them blend with their surroundings. This makes it possible for cougars to **ambush** animals four times their own size.

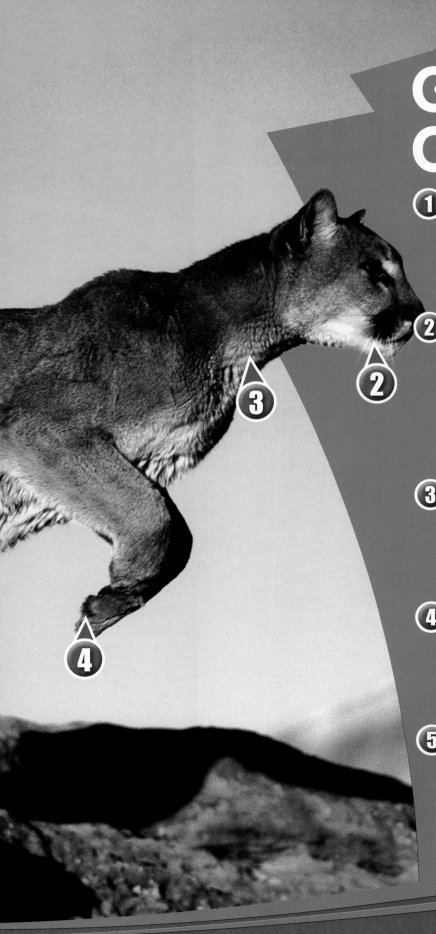

Getting Closer

① Coat

- Sandy-colored coat
- White throat, belly, and inside leg
- Black fur on tips of ears and tail

② Teeth

- Two long fangs, or canines, on the upper jaw and two on the lower
- Used to hook into prey to keep it from running away

③ Throat

- Purrs, hisses, and howls to communicate
- Cannot roar

④ Paws

- Paws about 3 to 4 inches (7.6 to 10 cm) across
- **Retractable** claws

⑤ Hind Legs

- Back legs longer than front legs
- Can jump 30 feet (9 m)
- Running speed of up to 35 miles (56 km) per hour

What Do Cougars Eat?

In North America, there are many large mammals for cougars to hunt. These prey animals include elk, deer, bighorn sheep, and moose. In South America, there are fewer large mammals. There, cougars eat small animals, such as mice, porcupines, and rabbits.

Most cougars need to eat one large animal every two weeks. Mothers providing food for their cubs must hunt more often. They may hunt every three days.

Cougars drag their kill to a place that is not often used by other animals. Then, they cover the animal with **brush**. Cougars return to eat the meat over many days.

Cougars sometimes eat porcupines. They try not to eat the sharp quills. However, quills that are swallowed soften in the cougar's stomach after about an hour.

FRESH FOOD

Cougars prefer to eat animals they have killed themselves. They rarely eat animals killed by other animals.

Cougar
Life Cycle

Adult cougars only live near each other during mating season. Mating season takes place over three or four weeks in the winter. Female cougars can have cubs at two-and-a-half years of age. Males are ready to mate when they are three or four years old. Cougars make a loud screeching noise when they are ready to mate.

Birth to 2 Weeks

Cougar cubs are born with their eyes closed. After two weeks, cubs can open their eyes, which are blue in color. Unlike adult cougars, cubs have dark spots on their coats. Newborn cubs weigh 1 pound (454 grams) or less.

Baby cougars are called cubs or kittens. They are born about three months after mating. This usually takes place in late winter or early spring. Most cougar litters have two to three cubs. Some have as many as six cubs. The mother raises the cubs without the father's help.

2 Years and Older

Cubs stay with their mother for up to two years. They learn to hunt and take care of themselves. Female cubs stay with their mother longer than male cubs. After leaving their mother, cubs often stay together for at least four months.

As adults, cougars live alone. Only mothers and cubs live as a family. Males allow only female cougars in their territory. Cougars can live up to 15 years in nature.

2 Weeks to 2 Years

For the first three to four months, cougar cubs drink their mother's milk. After six weeks, they can eat meat also. The spots on the cubs' coat fade after about six months. When the cubs reach about one year and four months of age, their eyes change to a greenish-yellow color.

Conservation of Cougars

There are about 50,000 cougars living in nature today. The number of cougars is much higher than most other big cat species. The fact that cougars travel alone and live across a wide range of habitats has helped the species to survive.

It has only been in the past 100 years that cougar numbers have increased. Cougar hunting almost brought the species to extinction in the late 1800s. Early settlers viewed cougars as threats to their livestock, and many cougars were shot by farmers and ranchers. Overkilling of cougars is still a threat to cougar numbers, along with loss of habitat. Many conservation groups, such as The Cougar Fund, are helping to raise awareness about the cougar and protect its habitats.

LOW NUMBERS

Cougars were classified as a near threatened species by the World Conservation Union in 2001.

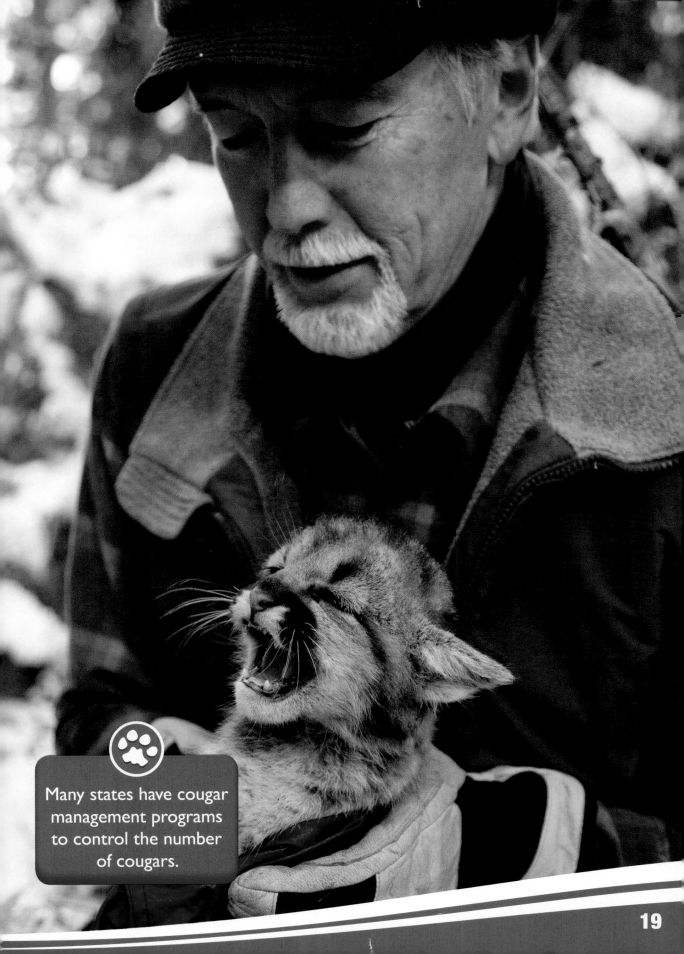

Many states have cougar management programs to control the number of cougars.

Myths and Legends

Indigenous North and South Americans have many legends about cougars. The people of the ancient **Inca** empire built temples in the shape of these cats and carved their image on rocks.

To the Inca, cougars represented strength. Cusco, the capital of the Inca empire, was built in the shape of a crouching cougar. The belly of the cougar was the main **plaza**. The river Tullumayo formed its spine, and the hill of Sacsayhuaman was its head.

The Aztecs of North America believed that scratching their chest with a cougar's bone would keep away death. Other groups put a cougar paw on a stick. They held the stick over a person's head to fend off evil.

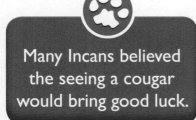

Many Incans believed the seeing a cougar would bring good luck.

Comparing Cats

When scientists identify animals, they group them with other animals that share similar characteristics. These groupings are called families. Cougars belong to the cat family, which is the same family as the common house cat. You can compare and contrast the characteristics of these two types of cats.

Materials Needed: You will need a piece of paper and a marker.

STEP 1 First, create a list of characteristics that cougars display. Think about the way they look, where they live, what they eat, and how they act. Then, create a similar list for house cats.

STEP 2 On a piece of paper, draw two large overlapping circles. At the top of one circle, write Cougars. At the top of the other circle, write House Cats. Where the two circles overlap, list the traits that cougars and house cats both have in common. In the outer circles, write the different features each cat has that the other does not.

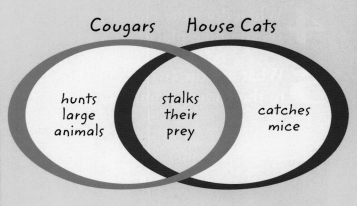

STEP 3 When you are done, you will be able to see all the features that make cougars similar to house cats, and also the traits that make them different. Many of the similar features that cougars and house cats share are shared by other members of the cat family. These characteristics help scientists group and identify different types of animals.

5 Know Your FACTS

Test your knowledge of cougars.

1 How did the cougars' ancestors first come to North America?

2 How large is a male cougar's territory?

3 What types of sounds do cougars make?

4 When does the cougar mating season take place?

5 What are the two major threats to the cougar population?

ANSWERS

1 They traveled from Asia across the Bering Land Bridge.

2 Between 30 and 386 square miles (78 and 1,000 sq. km)

3 Purring, hissing, and howling noises

4 3 or 4 weeks over winter

5 Overkilling and loss of habitat

Key Words

adaptations: adjustments to the natural environment

ambush: attack from a hidden position or by surprise

ancestor: a relative that lived long ago

Bering Land Bridge: a long, thin stretch of land that once connected Alaska to Siberia

brush: loose branches, leaves, and grass

extinction: no longer living any place on Earth

Guinness World Record: a guide to world records

habitat: the environment in which an animal lives

Inca: an ancient people who lived in South America; their empire lasted from the 1100s to 1533

indigenous: the first or original people, plants, or animals of a certain place

mammals: warm-blooded, live-born animals that have fur or hair, and drink milk from their mother

plaza: a public meeting place

predator: an animal that hunts other animals for food

prey: an animal that is hunted

retractable: capable of being drawn in

species: animals or plants that share certain features and can breed together

Index

Log on to www.av2books.com

AV[2] by Weigl brings you media enhanced books that support active learning. Go to www.av2books.com, and enter the special code found on page 2 of this book. You will gain access to enriched and enhanced content that supplements and complements this book. Content includes video, audio, weblinks, quizzes, a slide show, and activities.

AV[2] Online Navigation

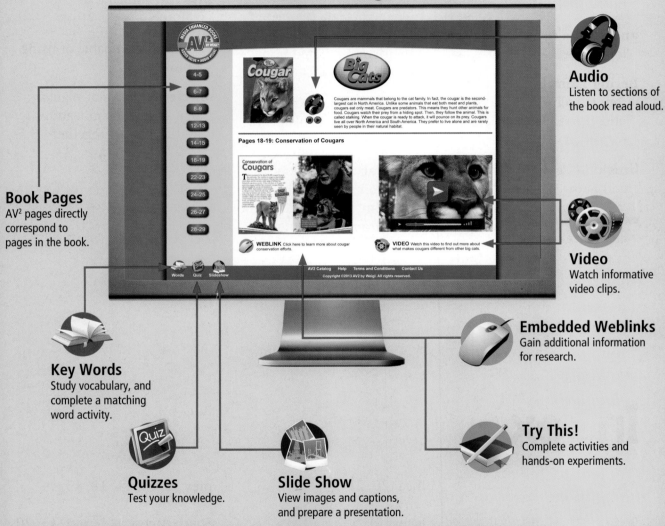

Audio
Listen to sections of the book read aloud.

Book Pages
AV[2] pages directly correspond to pages in the book.

Video
Watch informative video clips.

Key Words
Study vocabulary, and complete a matching word activity.

Embedded Weblinks
Gain additional information for research.

Quizzes
Test your knowledge.

Slide Show
View images and captions, and prepare a presentation.

Try This!
Complete activities and hands-on experiments.

AV[2] was built to bridge the gap between print and digital. We encourage you to tell us what you like and what you want to see in the future.

Sign up to be an AV[2] Ambassador at www.av2books.com/ambassador.